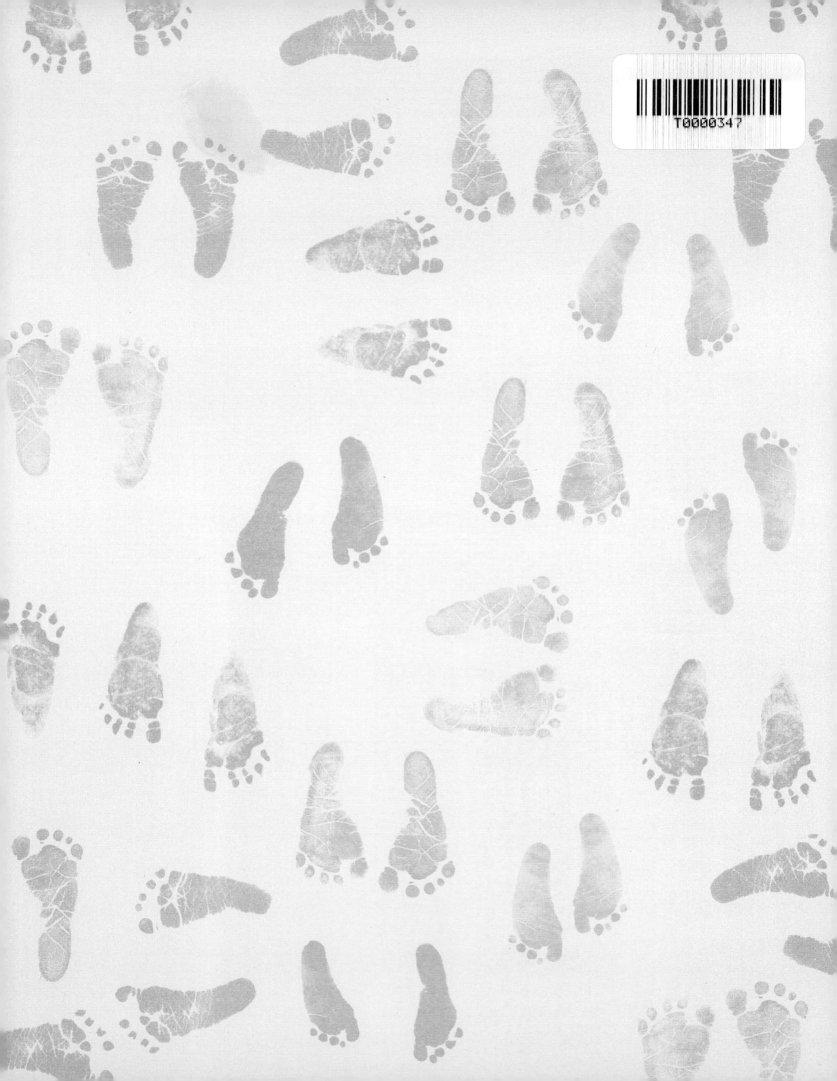

VIRGINIA WOULDN'T SLOW DOWN!

The Unstoppable Dr. Apgar and Her Life-Saving Invention

Carrie A. Pearson

Illustrated by **Nancy Carpenter**

Norton Young Readers

An Imprint of W. W. Norton & Company
Celebrating a Century of Independent Publishing

*To Taylor, Elle, and Sierra (aka "The Twisted Sisters"):
I'm honored to be your mom.*

*To my husband, Wally, for all the medical consults,
and to the Apgar family, thank you for sharing Ginny.*

—C.A.P.

*To my father, Whitney Carpenter (1938–2022), who had
the most wonderful sense of humor. I'm so lucky some of
it rubbed off on me.*

—N.C.

Photographs: (Apgar and brother in Professional Timeline; reproduction of signature in Sources) Mount Holyoke College Archives and Special Collections; (Apgar at work in Sources) Elizabeth Wilcox, Courtesy Archives & Special Collections, Columbia University Health Sciences Library.

For information about permission to reproduce selections from this book, write to Permissions, W. W. Norton & Company, Inc., 500 Fifth Avenue, New York, NY 10110

For information about special discounts for bulk purchases, please contact W. W. Norton Special Sales at specialsales@wwnorton.com or 800-233-4830

Manufacturing by Toppan Leefung
Book design by Hana Anouk Nakamura
Production manager: Delaney Adams

ISBN 978-1-324-00393-9

W. W. Norton & Company, Inc., 500 Fifth Avenue,
New York, N.Y. 10110
www.wwnorton.com

W. W. Norton & Company Ltd., 15 Carlisle Street, London W1D 3BS

1 2 3 4 5 6 7 8 9 0

Did you know that you took your first test just one minute after you were born?

The test showed doctors and nurses how healthy you were, if you could breathe on your own, or if you needed help—FAST!

The test was invented by Dr. Virginia Apgar in the 1940s. It helped save the lives of so many babies that it is still given to newborns around the world today. It has been said that every baby born in a hospital is seen through the eyes of Dr. Apgar.

But before she could invent the test, Dr. Apgar—or Ginny, as her friends and family called her—faced many hurdles.

Ginny's first hurdle
was being born a girl.

Girls raised in Ginny's time couldn't easily choose what kind of job they wanted. In those days, girls were often expected to wear dresses, learn how to be homemakers, and stay quiet.

That's the world Ginny grew up in.

But Ginny was different.

She WOULDN'T stay quiet. Her music, her laughter, and her questions filled the air.

She WASN'T interested in homemaking. In fact, her only low grade in school was in home economics.

She DIDN'T wear dresses all the time. She wore all sorts of outfits.

Ginny decided to become a doctor, even though most doctors in her time were men, and she'd never even seen a female doctor.

Maybe Ginny became curious about science from watching her father's experiments in his basement laboratory. Maybe she wished doctors could have cured her brothers. One died from tuberculosis, and the other had a painful skin condition. Maybe she believed she could do anything she put her mind to.

Ginny earned excellent grades in high school and was accepted into college. Four years later, she received another acceptance—to medical school—and took a giant step toward becoming a doctor. In medical school, she earned higher grades than almost everyone in her class.

Ginny didn't let being a girl slow her down.

Ginny's second hurdle? Money.

Then and now, going to college and medical school costs a lot. Ginny's parents couldn't pay for her schooling. She had to pay her own way.

So, while Ginny read, studied, and took tests, she also worked to pay her own bills.

She babysat.

She waited tables.

She even got a job catching stray cats on campus.

Each year, she added together the money she earned from work, scholarships that schools gave her for being a good student, and a little money from family and friends.

Each year, it was just enough to pay her bills.

Ginny carefully kept track of how much she owed people. She would pay them back when she earned her own money—when she became a doctor.

Ginny didn't let money troubles trip her up.

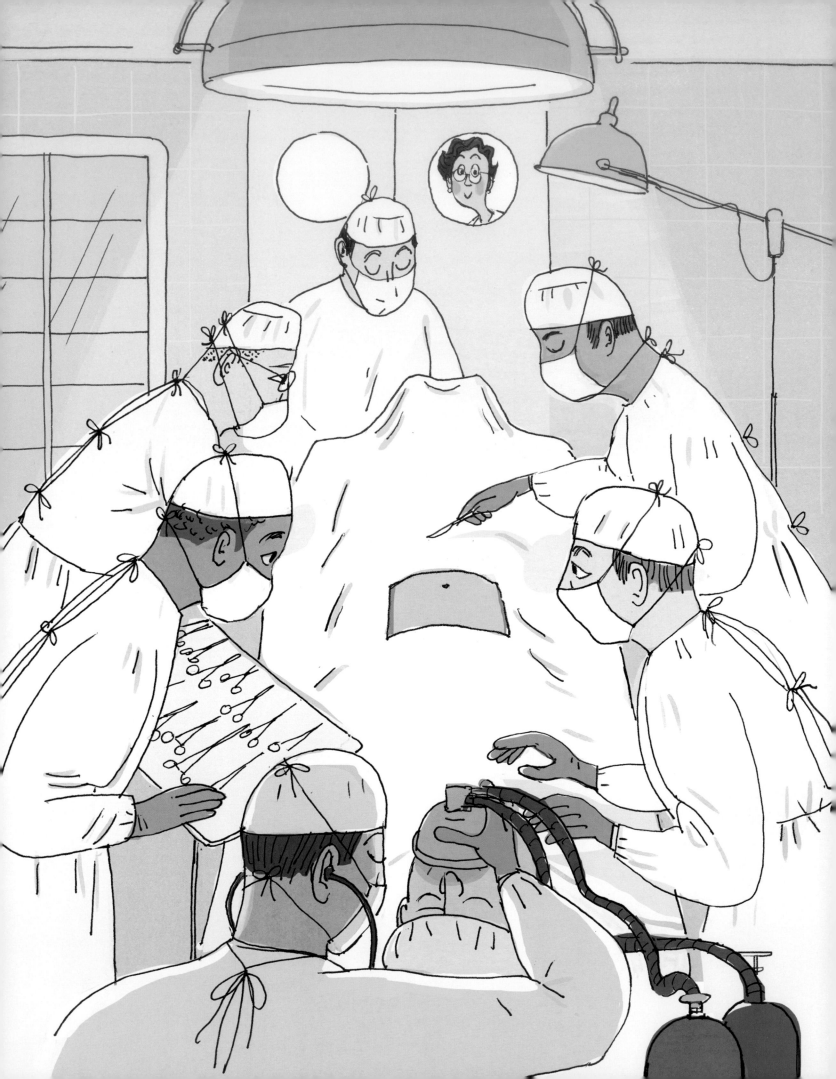

Ginny's third hurdle? Timing.

In 1933, Ginny finally earned her medical degree and a new title: Dr. Virginia Apgar. But she didn't want to stop there. She wanted to become a surgeon. Although this would mean more time and money for training, she was determined to do it.

But ten months into her training, Virginia changed course.

It was the time of the Great Depression, and people were so poor that they couldn't afford to pay doctors. Even if they could pay, there were few women doctors and even fewer women surgeons. Many people might feel uncomfortable going to one practicing on her own. Would Virginia earn enough money as a surgeon to pay her bills?

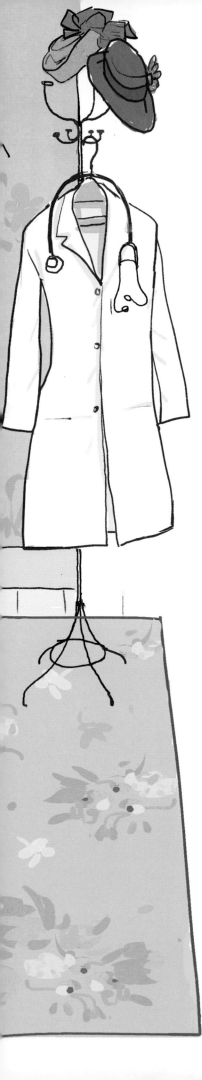

A teacher suggested that Virginia become an anesthesiologist—a doctor who keeps patients safe and free of pain during surgery or other procedures. Anesthesiology was a new field, and more anesthesiologists were needed. Virginia would be among the first anesthesiologists in the United States.

It was hard to give up her dream of becoming a surgeon, but Virginia decided that this was a better path for her. She stepped to her next starting line.

Virginia learned from nurses who had been giving medicines for pain and from the few anesthesiologists in the country.

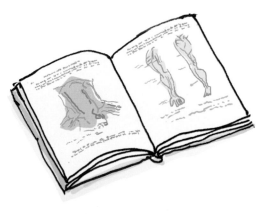

In 1938, Virginia became the second board-certified female anesthesiologist in the United States. She took a new job in a busy hospital in New York City.

Virginia made the most of her opportunities.

One of Virginia's jobs as an anesthesiologist was to monitor mothers' pain during the delivery of new babies.

What she found in the delivery room shocked her. Many babies weren't breathing well after they were born and needed help. But doctors and nurses were focused on mothers' health and safety. Without attention, many newborns didn't survive.

At that time, doctors didn't agree on who was responsible for newborns and what were the best ways to treat them. What was "normal" breathing and what wasn't? Should they give oxygen, or not? How and when should doctors do something to help? Or should they let babies who had trouble breathing just keep trying on their own?

That's the world babies were born into in 1949.

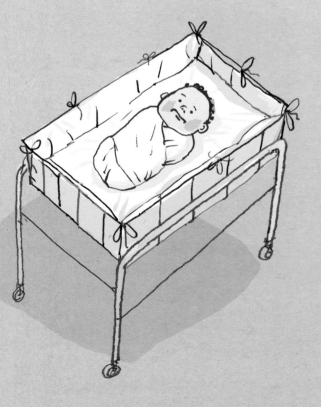

Because of her training as an anesthesiologist, Virginia knew how to help. If a baby wasn't breathing, she might carefully clear his mouth with suction, insert a tiny tube to open his airway, or give him oxygen through a small face mask. Terribly long seconds might pass. Would the baby breathe on his own? Would he live?

Most often, the baby's chest would start to rise and fall normally. His skin would become a healthy color. He would begin to move his little arms and legs, and his heartbeat would grow stronger. This baby would live.

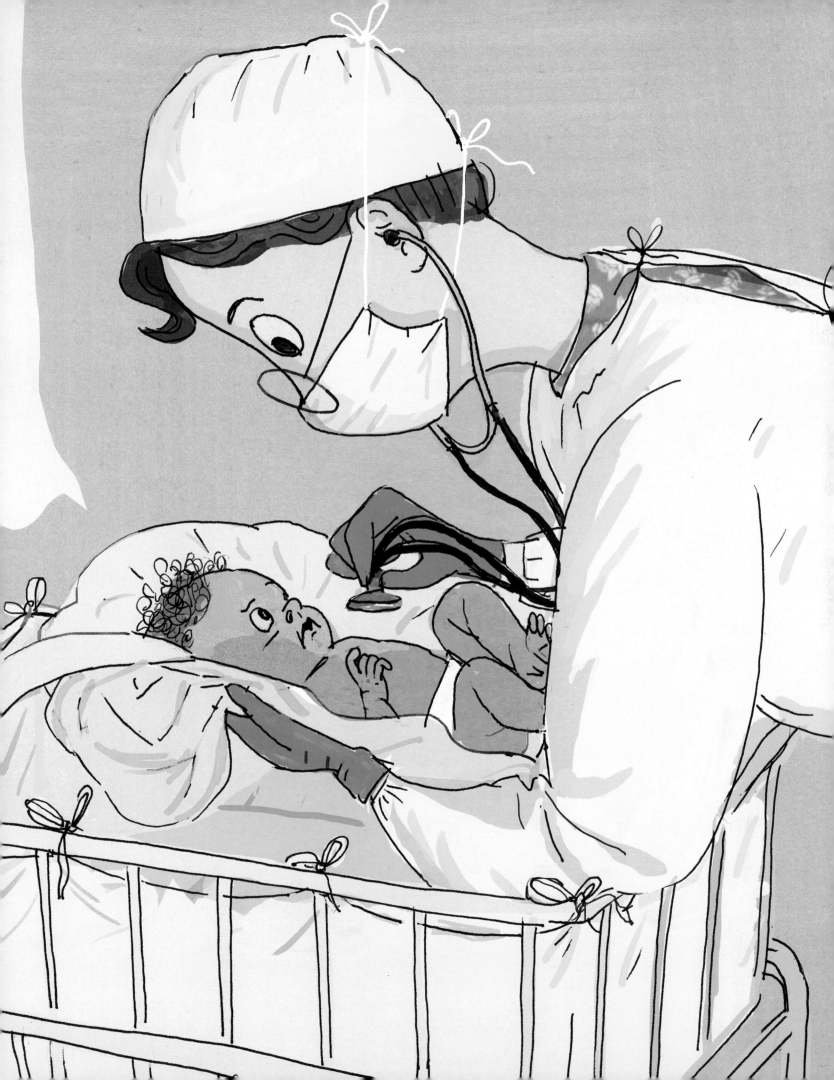

Virginia knew the medical world needed to change how it cared for newborns. But why should other doctors listen to her?

She wasn't a doctor who delivered babies (an obstetrician).

She wasn't a doctor who cared for babies (a pediatrician).

She was a new kind of doctor (an anesthesiologist).

And she was a woman.

Virginia faced her biggest hurdle yet.

One day, a young doctor in training asked Virginia how someone could quickly measure the health of a newborn. Virginia said, "That's easy! You'd do it this way." She picked up the nearest piece of paper. She wrote down five signs of health that anesthesiologists use to be sure their patients are safe during surgery: heart rate, respiratory effort, muscle tone, reflex irritability, and color.

Virginia realized that babies could be tested right after birth on those same five signs of health: heartbeat, breathing, muscle strength, if the baby moved away from pain, and if the baby was a healthy color.

She assigned a number to each sign of health. Babies who scored high numbers on the test were healthy. Babies who scored low needed help—FAST! Virginia's test took a question that was hard to answer—"Is the baby healthy?"—and gave it a score that could be counted and compared.

Any nurse or doctor in the delivery room could quickly and easily give this test to newborns. Mothers would still be safe, but now the focus would be on babies, too. More babies would be paid attention to! More babies would be helped! More babies would be saved!

In the months to come, Virginia and a team of researchers performed the test on many newborns, collected their scores, and used the data to show how the test helped babies.

Once Virginia realized how she and others could change how newborns were cared for, she WOULDN'T stay quiet. In fact, she talked about the score and babies to anyone who would listen.

She WASN'T willing to waste any time. In fact, she walked so fast that people had to hurry to keep up. She spoke so quickly that she was sometimes hard to understand.

She DIDN'T forget how humor, encouragement, and being generous support people as they learn. In fact, she loved to tell jokes and help students feel better when they made mistakes. Because there were no textbooks about anesthesiology, she wrote a guide and used her own body to teach students.

Her scoring system caught on. By the early 1960s, hospitals across the United States and other countries tracked, measured, and compared newborns using Virginia's score. No one wanted low scores from their delivery rooms, so doctors and nurses worked harder to help babies.

Even when she took a break from the hospital, Virginia didn't rest. She planted gardens and cut and hauled wood for her fireplace. She took fishing trips all over the world, played music in quartets, and made string instruments with her own busy hands. She still didn't like to cook and she often burned her food. She drove her car fast. She even had a special gun that shot quarters at tollbooths so she wouldn't have to slow down!

Meanwhile, the scoring system continued to help newborns. In 1961, Virginia received a letter from a doctor who told her that his training program used the letters of Virginia's last name as a way for people to remember what to score.

A for Appearance *(Is the baby's skin a healthy color?)*

P for Pulse *(Is the baby's heart beating normally?)*

G for Grimace *(Does the baby pull away when poked?)*

A is for Activity *(Does the baby use its muscles?)*

R is for Respiration *(Does the baby have a strong cry?)*

Virginia said, "I chortled aloud when I saw the epigram. It is very clever and certainly original!"

Virginia didn't let being a girl slow her down. She didn't let money problems trip her up. She made the most of her opportunities. She was a doctor, a scientist, and the inventor of a test that has helped save the lives of millions of babies around the world—and still does every single day.

It is likely that someone tested you with the APGAR Score when you were born. It's even possible that it showed the people caring for you that you needed help right away. Perhaps someday, the person who gives the APGAR Score—and saves a baby's life—will be you.

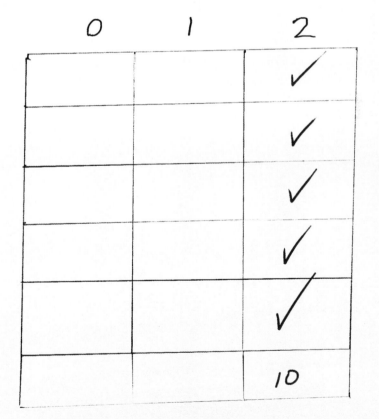

	0	1	2
Appearance			✓
Pulse			✓
Grimace			✓
Activity			✓
Respiration			✓
total			10

AUTHOR'S NOTE

When each of our three daughters was born, I waited to hear her APGAR Score because I knew it was an important measurement of her health, but until I saw a picture of Dr. Apgar one day, I knew nothing of the woman who invented the test. Her generous smile and the twinkle in her eye drew me in. As I researched Virginia's life, I wondered what made her the kind of person to accomplish all that she did. I discovered that she was a unique blend of persistence, charisma, and resiliency, with a large dash of good humor. For all these reasons and more, Virginia Apgar is my heroine, and I hope she will become yours.

VIRGINIA was born in Westfield, New Jersey, on June 7, 1909. Her father, Charles Emory Apgar, was Virginia's "greatest inspiration." He loved music and science—particularly astronomy. He helped crack a German "U-boat" (submarine) code and was responsible for closing a German spy station during World War I. Thomas Edison repeatedly tried to recruit Charles to work for him but was unsuccessful.

Virginia's mother, Helen Clarke Apgar, managed their household and family. However, according to Virginia, Helen "expressed the wish to have been a businesswoman in her younger days—unheard of in those times." The Apgar family suffered a significant loss when their first child, Charles, died of tuberculosis at age three.

Their second-born child, Lawrence, became an Ivy League college professor and a world-class organist and musician. Virginia said she felt like an underachiever in comparison! Lawrence had a type of ichthyosis, a genetically inherited skin disorder.

One of Mr. Apgar's sisters and a teacher, Aunt May, lived with Virginia's family for several formative years. She and Virginia "clicked like a key in a lock," Virginia said.

Virginia grew up in a neighborhood of boys and felt this was one of her "childhood assets." She participated on all their teams, was taught "man's style" tennis, and excelled in baseball. She expanded her many activities while at Mount Holyoke College, including playing on several sports teams. She was in the drama club and the orchestra—and she worked in between it all! Virginia kept meticulous notes about her spending and the few people she owed for their limited financial support.

When Virginia entered medical school in 1929, only 1 in 10 students was a woman. Until 1975, the American College of Surgeons admitted only 5 or fewer women per year. Virginia secured a surgical internship and completed a challenging year despite these odds.

Therefore, it is hard to imagine how difficult it must have been for her to decide to pursue anesthesia instead of surgery. Training opportunities for anesthesia were scarce, and almost all of them were unpaid. Her peer group would be the one other board-certified female anesthesiologist in the United States.

But the discovery of better anesthetics led to more surgeries, and hospitals needed more well-trained anesthesiologists. Virginia charged ahead. At the age of twenty-eight, she began her career in anesthesia and quickly moved into leadership, teaching, recruitment, administrative, and medical practice roles. Hoping to decrease the newborn death rate, Virginia created the quick, reproducible health assessment that came to be known as the APGAR Score. It was "the first clinical method to recognize the newborn's needs as a patient."

Virginia and her colleagues focused on why some babies had low APGAR Scores. They found that certain medicines given to mothers during delivery helped with their pain but affected their babies' heartrate, breathing, and responses. This information led to changes in medications given to mothers during childbirth.

The APGAR Score laid the foundation for an increased understanding of newborn health, the rise of neonatology (medical care of newborn infants, especially ill or premature babies) as a medical field, neonatal intensive care units, and ways to monitor the health of newborns prior, during, and after delivery. The APGAR Score changed the decisions doctors and nurses made about how to care for newborns.

Virginia was instrumental in the maternal and fetal health movement with the National Health Foundation/March of Dimes. She coauthored a groundbreaking book for parents about neonatal and newborn health problems called *Is My Baby All Right?* Throughout her career, Virginia attended or witnessed over 17,000 deliveries and trained over 100 anesthesiology students.

Virginia was sure of her abilities and forthright, yet she showed humility and graciousness. Above all, she treated others with respect and kindness. A colleague and friend said, "One grateful parent remembers how Apgar carried a child who was afraid of elevators up nine flights of stairs to surgery." Another said, "Virginia Apgar was so devoted to the cause of infant health that even during the last year of her life (when her own health was failing), she traveled 83,000 miles and visited three continents" to talk about the issues.

Virginia traveled worldwide, shooting Super 8 movies, and snapping pictures with her camera. In her late fifties, she learned to fly single-engine airplanes in case a plane in which she flew had trouble. She loved to collect stamps, and her image, fittingly, was featured on a United States Postal Service stamp.

PROFESSIONAL TIMELINE

Born: **June 7, 1909**, to Helen Clarke Apgar and Charles Emory Apgar in Westfield, New Jersey.

College: **1925–1929**, Mount Holyoke College, zoology major.

Medical school: **1929–1933**, Columbia University's College of Physicians and Surgeons (fourth in her class).

Board-certified in anesthesiology: **1939** (second woman certified in the United States).

First woman with a professorship in anesthesiology at the College of Physicians and Surgeons at Columbia University: **1949**.

APGAR Score: Created **1949**, presented **1952**, published **1953**.

Masters of Public Health in genetics at Johns Hopkins University: **1958–1959**.

Virginia Apgar, about age three, and her brother, Lawrence.

Executive medical staff at National Foundation-March of Dimes as chief of congenital malformations: **1959**.

Distinguished Service Award, American Society of Anesthesiologists: **1959**.

Scoring system renamed and shared by Dr. L. Joseph Butterfield using A P G A R as a mnemonic (or backronym): **1962**.

Distinguished Service Award, American Society of Anesthesiologists; Elizabeth Blackwell Medal, American Medical Women's Association: **1966**.

Lecturer and clinical professor of pediatrics (teratology) at Cornell University College of Medicine; first to hold a faculty post in that subspecialty of pediatrics: **1965–1973**.

Honorary doctorate from New Jersey College of Medicine and Dentistry: **1967**.

Director of Basic Medical Research at National Foundation-March of Dimes: **1967–1968**.

Vice President for Medical Affairs at National Foundation-March of Dimes: **1971**.

Published book, *Is My Baby All Right?*, written with Joan Beck: **1972**.

Woman of the Year, *Ladies Home Journal*; Ralph Waters Award, American Society of Anesthesiologists: **1973**.

First woman to receive the Gold Medal for Distinguished Achievement in Medicine from the College of Physicians and Surgeons, Columbia University: **1973**.

Died: **August 7, 1974**, in New York City, age sixty-five.

Third woman doctor honored on a United States Postal Service stamp: **1994**.

Inducted into the National Women's Hall of Fame: **1995**.

SOURCES

This book is based on personal interviews with and reviews by Virginia Apgar's nephew, Charles E. (Scotty) Apgar; Virginia's personal papers and memorabilia housed at the Virginia Apgar Collection at Mount Holyoke College; and published sources and archives, the most important of which were the National Institute of Health (NIH), National Library of Medicine, the Virginia Apgar Papers and an autobiographical overview written by Dr. Apgar, dated June 21, 1974.

"You just had to be twice as smart as the men in your class."

Virginia ☺